CO-BUY-043

more adventures of spider

West African Folk Tales

Retold by
Joyce Cooper Arkhurst

Illustrated by Jerry Pinkney

SCHOLASTIC INC.
New York Toronto London Auckland Sydney

To Cecile Nanaba
whose forefathers
knew these stories

No part of this publication may be reproduced in whole or in part, or stored in a retrieval system, or transmitted in any form or by any means, electronic, mechanical, photocopying, recording, or otherwise, without written permission of the publisher. For information regarding permission, write to Scholastic Inc., 730 Broadway, New York, NY 10003.

ISBN 0-590-33817-X

Text copyright © 1972 by Joyce Cooper Arkhurst. Illustrations copyright © 1972 by Scholastic Inc. All rights reserved. Published by Scholastic Inc.

12 11 10 9 8 7 6 5 4 3 2   8 9/8 0 1 2 3/9

Special Words from Africa

Ashanti
a-SHAN-ti

A region of Ghana where *kente* — a bright-colored cloth — is made.

calabash
CAL-a-bash

A gourd dried out and used to store liquids or split to make ladles.

cassava
cass-AH-vah

A root vegetable; tastes like potatoes, but it is much larger — sometimes two feet long.

fufu
foo-foo

A kind of dumpling made by pounding cassava or plantain with a heavy stick in a deep wooden bowl. These are called "mortar and pestle."

kenkey

A cake made of white cornmeal. It is sliced and eaten with peppery stews or fish.

kente
KEN-tee

Cloth woven by hand. It is made of hand-dyed silk and cotton thread. Kente is woven in long strips. The strips are sewn together to make wide pieces of cloth. People wear kente when they go to parties. The colors are bright gold, green, blue, orange, black, and white.

Lake Bosumtwi
bo-SOOM-chee

A sacred lake in Ashanti where people believe water spirits live.

Nyame
nee-AH-mee

The God of the Sky. The supreme God who rules all things.

palaver house
pa-LAH-ver

Palaver means "talking." The palaver house is a small open house in the village where men gather to chat in the evenings.

palm wine

A drink made from the sap of a palm tree.

pepper

Hot green, red, and yellow peppers used in cooking. This term seldom refers to black pepper.

plantain
PLAN-tin

A fruit that looks like a very big banana. It is fried or boiled or pounded into fufu. It is not eaten raw.

Introduction

All over West Africa, people tell stories about Spider. Most of the stories in this book come from Ghana, a country on the coast of West Africa. They are called "Spider Stories."

When you know the kind of stories people tell, you get some idea of what kind of people they are. You will notice in these stories that West Africans are very particular about three things: cleanliness, hospitality, and good manners. Everyone bathes at least once every day, and sometimes two or three times. A stranger must be made welcome, and food must be shared.

But, as in all countries, not everyone does as he is supposed to do. West Africans noticed this too, and that is why they made up the character of Spider. Spider is like some people.

He is lazy and very, very greedy. He loves to play. He hates to work. He is full of tricks, and he is often naughty. But he is funny and lovable too.

Let us begin, then, the telling of our stories. We will start the way storytellers in Ghana often begin to tell a story: "I am the storyteller, and here is my story. Do not believe it, for it never really happened. It is only a story. I am the storyteller, and here is my story."

Spider and the Magic Cooking Pot

In the land of Ashanti, where Spider lived, there is neither winter nor summer. Instead, there is a dry time and a rainy time; and during the dry time, it is very hot and there is no rain at all.

ONCE long ago, before your grandmother was a little girl, there was a very long dry time. The rain did not come and there was little food for people to eat. Spider was hungry, and so were his wife and his children.

One day, Spider set out to look for something to eat. He walked for a day and a night. At last he came to the shore of the sea. He shaded his eyes and looked out over the water. There, a little way from the shore, was a tiny island. It had just one tree on it. The tree stood near the edge of the water and was covered with large green coconuts.

Spider's heart pounded. If only he could reach the island! Those beautiful coconuts would be filled with milk, and their meat would be fine and sweet.

Suddenly Spider saw a small boat lying on the shore. He pushed it into the sea and rowed toward the island.

"What a strange little island," Spider said to himself when he reached the shore. "There seems to be magic about it."

In no time, Spider climbed the tree and began to pick the huge nuts. He tried to drop them into the little boat. But each nut fell into the sea instead. He tried again and again, but the nuts splashed down into the water and disappeared.

Finally, Spider could stand it no longer. He jumped into the water. Perhaps he could find one or two nuts. To his surprise, he sank

deeper and deeper. Something pulled him
down — down into the blue-green water until
he reached the very bottom of the sea.

There, in front of him, was a little house
made of sea shells, and in the doorway stood
an old, old man.

"My name is Thunder," said the old man, "and I am king here. Who are you, and why have you come to my island?"

Spider told Thunder about the dry season, and how he and his family had nothing to eat. The old man felt sorry for Spider and kindly offered to help him. He went inside the little house made of sea shells. In a moment he returned carrying a small black cooking pot.

"Take this pot," he said, "and rub it. Then wait a moment, and say to it, 'Do whatever you would do for the old man Thunder.' The pot will give you all the food you can eat."

Spider was overjoyed. He rubbed the pot and said, "Do whatever you would do for the old man Thunder!"

At once, the pot was filled with delicious food. There was steaming rice and cassava and meat. Spider ate until he could eat no more. And then he started the long journey back to his village, thinking how happy his family would be.

But as he got closer to home, he began to change his mind. And the closer he got, the more his mind changed.

"Why should I share this wonderful pot with anyone?" Spider said to himself. "I shall hide it in a secret place and keep it all for myself."

And that is just what Spider did. He took the magic pot deep into the forest. He dug a hole and put the pot in it and covered the hole with leaves. At night, when everyone was asleep, he took the pot out and ate to his heart's content.

Time passed. Spider's eldest son, Kuma, began to notice that Spider was getting fatter. He was getting fatter and fatter, while everyone else got thinner and thinner. How could this be? Kuma decided to find out.

Kuma turned himself into a fly and followed Spider wherever he went. Of course, he soon discovered the magic pot. He discovered the magic words too.

One day when Spider was out, Kuma told

Aso, his mother, about the wonderful pot. Aso took the pot from its hiding place. She rubbed it and waited a moment. Then she said, "Do for me whatever you would do for the old man Thunder." At once the pot was filled with food. Aso and all her children had a delicious meal.

Then Aso took the pot to the marketplace in the middle of the village. She asked it to feed the whole village, because everyone there was hungry. The little pot tried to do so, but this was too much for it. Alas, it melted away and disappeared altogether.

How angry Spider would be! Aso and Kuma decided not to tell Spider what had happened. That night when Spider went to get the pot, he could not find it. He looked everywhere. Poor Spider went to bed hungry.

The very next morning, Spider hurried to the island, to ask the old man for another pot. He traveled very fast, and soon came to the same island and the same small boat as before. He rowed to the island and jumped into the water. Down he went to the bottom of the sea. There, as before, was the little shell house with the old man standing in the doorway.

Spider told him the story of the lost pot. He asked the old man to help him again.

"Did your wife and your children enjoy the good food from my pot?" asked the old man.

Spider was ashamed. He could not answer — he only looked down at his feet.

Without a word, the old man went into the house. When he came back, he was carrying a large stick. He gave it to Spider and told him to rub it just as he had done with the pot.

"And then," said the old man, "you must say, 'Do for me what you would do for the old man Thunder.'"

Spider took the stick eagerly, hardly stopping to thank the old man. As soon as he was in the boat, he rubbed the stick and cried, "Do for me what you would do for the old man Thunder!"

At once the stick began to beat him.

"Stop! Stop! Stop!" cried Spider, but the stick paid no attention. It continued to spank him soundly.

"Stop that, you rascal!" Spider shouted. But the stick kept right on spanking him. It gave him a sound thrashing. At last, Spider jumped straight out of the boat and into the cool water. He swam back to land as fast as he could. He never looked back. He never saw the stick or the island or the old man Thunder again. And he never found another magic pot.

How Spider Invited Turtle to Dinner

People in Africa love proverbs. A proverb is a wise saying that tells us something about life. I am sure that you know some proverbs already, like:

The early bird gets the worm.

And here is an African proverb:

He who sows nettles does not reap roses.
(Nettles are small green plants that sting.) Our next story ends with this proverb. When you have read the story, you can guess what the proverb means.

ONE EVENING Spider cooked himself a delicious dinner. He was very pleased. "What a delicious dinner I have cooked!" said Spider happily. "I can hardly wait to taste it."

He set the dinner on his little table. There was a big pot of chicken stew, some baked plantain, and bean cakes. There was a bowl of soup with meat, and fried fish with a special cornmeal cake called "kenkey." Spider's mouth watered, and his eyes sparkled.

He was about to eat when he heard a knock at the door. Spider waited a minute. Knock. Knock. Knock.

"What a nuisance," thought Spider, "just when I'm having my dinner." He opened the door, and there stood old Turtle. Turtle was very tired and covered with dust. He had come a long way from his house near Lake Bosumtwi.

"Good evening, Spider," said Turtle. "I have been walking all day, and I am so tired. May I come and rest awhile?"

Spider was very annoyed, but he could not refuse. What would people say? And so he politely asked Turtle to come in. As soon as he got inside, Turtle saw Spider's dinner spread out on the table.

"Oh, Spider," he exclaimed, "my very favorite dish! Fried fish with peppers and kenkey."

"How annoying," thought Spider to himself. "Now I shall have to invite him to dinner." For even greedy Spider knew he must invite his guest to eat with him. So Spider smiled a cross little smile and asked Turtle to share his dinner. Turtle was delighted, of course, for he was hungry as well as tired. He waited politely for Spider to ask him to come to the table.

But Spider did not ask him. Instead, he left the room. When he came back, he was carrying a large towel.

"Dear Turtle, you are covered with dust. I

am sure you would like to take a bath before you eat," said Spider. "Behind my house, down a short path through the forest, you will find a small river. Take this towel and bathe yourself quickly."

Turtle was glad to take a bath. He splashed about in the clear, clean water and thought of the tasty fish he would have.

But when he returned, Turtle was surprised to see that Spider was already eating. Half of the corn cakes were gone, and Spider was taking great spoonfuls of fish.

"Ah, there you are," shouted Spider. "But, my dear Turtle, you cannot possibly eat at my table. Look at your dirty feet. You will have to wash them again."

Turtle looked down at his feet. Alas, it was true. He had run up the path from the river so fast that his feet were covered with dust. Down to the river he ran. He jumped into the water and washed as fast as he could. By now he was hungrier than ever. Turtle dried his feet quickly and rushed back to the house, trying to walk only on his toes.

By the time he reached the table, he noticed that all the fish and nearly half of the chicken were gone. Just as he was about to sit down, Spider exlaimed, "Turtle, HOW can you be so careless? Your feet are still dirty! You will just have to wash them again, for in my country you cannot eat with dirty feet."

Turtle looked at his feet. Sure enough, they were very dirty indeed. He would have to wash them again. Turtle ran down to the river. He wanted to get back while there was still some dinner left. He was in such a hurry, he splashed water all around. And this time, as he went back through the forest, he was careful to walk only on the grass. When he got back, his feet were quite clean, but the food was all gone! Not a scrap was left. Spider had eaten the very last mouthful.

But that is not the end of the story.

Some time later, Spider went to market far

from his house. He wanted to buy oranges or bananas or fried plantain. But when he got to market he didn't have a penny. He had lost his money.

Just when the sun was setting, Spider found himself in front of the house of Turtle. Now, Turtle was sitting in his doorway, as people do of an early evening, and he saw Spider slowly walking past.

"Ah," said Turtle, "good evening, Spider. You look rather tired today. Come into my little house and rest."

Turtle's house was made of soft red clay and it was cool and pleasant. Spider was very glad to sit down.

"Dinner is almost ready," said Turtle. "It just happens I have prepared your very favorite dish — chicken and rice." (Turtle knew that Spider loved chicken and rice.) "Please stay and eat dinner with me."

Spider was delighted.

"Excuse me," Turtle said. "I must put the

dinner on the table." With that he left the room. Soon, he called Spider to come and eat. Spider jumped up to follow him. Much to his surprise, Turtle took him to the shore of Lake Bosumtwi.

"Just follow me," Turtle said. "As you know, in my country, people are most comfortable in the water." With that, Turtle jumped into the water and disappeared.

Good heavens! Turtle had set the dinner on a table at the very bottom of the lake! Spider could see Turtle and all the food through the clear, deep water. Turtle was already eating.

Spider jumped into the water after Turtle. What was this? He could *not* sink to the bottom. Every time Spider pushed his head under the water, it simply popped up. He pushed his arms under, but his feet stuck out. He pushed his feet under, and his arms stuck out. He kicked his feet like a paddle wheel and tried to push the rest of him under, but he was just too light. Nothing, *nothing* would make him sink to the bottom of the lake. He stayed right up on the top.

All this time, Turtle was eating.

Spider grew angrier and angrier. Also hungrier. "I must think of something," he told himself. And, at last, he thought of something. He jumped out of the water and onto the shore. Quickly Spider put on his jacket. He filled the pockets with the largest stones he could find. Then he went back to the water. Sure enough, this time, he sank right down to the bottom, and landed in front of his place at the table.

"Really, Spider," exclaimed Turtle, "you cannot sit at the table with your jacket on. In my country, people do not eat with their jackets on. We think it is very rude."

Naturally, Spider did not want anyone to think he was rude. So he took his jacket off. No sooner did he lay it down than he floated right back up to the top of the water, and there he stayed. Poor Spider. He never got down again to the beautiful table at the bottom of Lake Bosumtwi.

As for Turtle, he simply smiled and went on eating, until every morsel of food was gone. And then he said quietly to himself, "He who plants nettles does not reap roses."

How Spider Lost His Whiskers

Years and years ago, Spider had a long black beard. It was thick and curly, and he was very proud of it. He thought his face looked especially fancy — and wise, besides, like that of an old man. All that was long ago. Now Spider has no beard at all. His chin is as smooth as an egg, and this is how it came to be so.

ONCE upon a time, Spider and his friend Antelope lived together in a little clay house. The roof was made of prickly thatch that hung like a fringe around the edges. Curtains hung in the windows. They kept out the hot sun in the daytime, and the moonlight at night.

Every morning, Antelope got up bright and early. He swept the floor and made the beds.

He cooked the breakfast and washed the dishes. Then he swept the little yard in front of their house until it was smooth and clean. All this time, lazy Spider did nothing at all. He sat up in bed smiling splendidly. He yawned loudly while Antelope swept the floor. He drank tea while Antelope washed the dishes.

At last, Antelope grew tired of all this, and he complained to Spider, "All day long I work in the house while you do nothing at all. You sleep while I cook and clean. Then you drink tea while I sweep the yard. In the afternoon, you go out and visit your friends. I do not like it. From now on you must do your share of the work."

"You are quite right, dear Antelope," answered Spider sweetly. "I agree to share the housework with you. But I cannot start today, for I am going to buy a farm! I will grow food on it — enough for both of us. You will see. Only give me time to find a really good farm."

Do you think Spider bought a farm?

Seven days passed. Nothing happened. And so again, Antelope told Spider he must do his share of the work. He was so angry that his little brown tail shook.

"I am so sorry," said Spider. "I forgot to tell you. I am going to get married, and then we will have someone to help us both with our work. Please be patient, Antelope. Only give me time to find a really good wife."

Do you think Spider got married?

No, he did not. He did not buy a farm, and he did not get married either. Instead he kept right on being lazy. He slept late and ate much. In the afternoon, he went swimming and sang songs and ran races with his friends. At dinnertime he came home and ate until his stomach nearly burst.

Antelope grew angrier and angrier. All his friends laughed at him and said how foolish he was to live with Spider.

"I'll think of a way to teach him a lesson," said Antelope. He sat under a banana tree and thought and thought and thought. At last he had an idea! "Aha!" Antelope said to himself, "I know! Spider loves to sleep and loves to play, but most of all he loves to eat." It was Spider's greediness that gave Antelope his idea. What a good idea it was! All day long Antelope smiled to himself whenever he thought of it.

Late that night when Spider came home, Antelope was waiting for him.

"Good evening, Spider," said Antelope politely. "Look, I have brought you some fresh palm wine from the finest palm tree of all. Would you like to drink a little before you go to bed?"

Spider had had enough to eat and drink already, but he could not resist. He took a large calabash and filled it to the very top with the sharp, sweet palm wine, and then he drank every drop. When he finished, he was so full he hardly knew what was up and what was down. So he jumped into bed and fell asleep.

It was the season of the full moon, and in

Africa the moon is very bright and looks as though you could reach right up and touch it. Antelope knew that late at night, when the moon reached the very highest corner of the sky, it would shine right into Spider's room.

Antelope tiptoed slowly, softly into Spider's bedroom. He was so silent that even a little gecko sitting in the doorway did not hear his footsteps. Quietly Antelope went to Spider's window and pulled away the curtain. The moonlight shone squarely in the middle of Spider's window and fell across Spider's face. Soon, Spider began to stir. His eyes opened and closed. Finally he looked up, and what did he see? A great round white thing hanging in the center of his window! Do you know what he thought it was? Have we not told you Spider liked to eat better than anything?

"Oh!" shouted Spider, who was not quite awake. "A big bowl of rice is sitting right in my window! It is the biggest bowl of rice in the whole world!"

And before he had a chance to look carefully, and before he knew quite what he was doing, Spider jumped straight through the window toward the great white bowl in the sky. He tried to catch it with all his eight arms and legs. His hair twirled all around his head. His thick curly beard got tangled up in the prickly thatch that hung down from the roof. It would not come loose!

Spider tugged at it with all his might. Snap! Snap! Snap! Spider's beard *came right off*. Oof! Spider fell to the ground. He shouted so loudly that everyone in the village woke up. People came from all directions to see what on earth had happened. They found Spider sitting under his window rubbing his chin, and Antelope laughing so hard he could not stand up.

When they heard what happened, the people shook their heads and scolded Spider for being so greedy. As for Spider, he was a *little* ashamed of himself. He smiled foolishly and promised to do his share of the work from that day on. Do you think he really did?

Well, maybe he did, and maybe he didn't. But one thing is certain. To this day, his whiskers have never come back, and his chin is as smooth as the moon herself.

How Spider Brought Weaving to Ashanti

In Ashanti, West Africa, the village weavers make a special cloth called "kente." It is pronounced "ken-tee." Kente is woven in long strips of bright colors — gold and green and blue and orange, and people wear it when they go to parties.

No one knows just who first learned to weave cloth, but it must have been long, long ago. And so the people of Ashanti made up a story that tells how men learned first to spin a thread, and then to weave cloth. Who do you think gave them such a good idea? Why, Spider, of course! He didn't really mean to. It was purely accidental.

EVERY Wednesday Spider and Opuro (that is the name for Tree Bear) went to market to sell their goods. Spider sold tobacco and Opuro sold salt. They carried their goods on their heads (as people do in Africa) and spread them out for customers to see. Now, people bought much more salt than tobacco, and so Opuro had much more money than Spider at the end of the day. You can imagine how Spider felt about that.

"Why should *he* have more money than *I* have?" said Spider spitefully. He was so jealous that one day, when Opuro was not looking, he stole every bag of Opuro's salt!

When Opuro saw Spider with many bags of salt, he guessed just what had happened.

"*You* have stolen my salt," he cried. "You will have to come to the chief, for I am going to ask him for a judgment. Then we will see whom this salt really belongs to." And so the day for the chief's judgment was set.

Early on the morning of the trial, Spider opened one of the bags of salt. He took a whole handful and rubbed it into his hair. Spider's hair was curly then, and so most of the salt stayed there.

When it was time for the chief to decide, Spider stood before him. "Oh, Chief," he said, "look into my hair and into Opuro's hair, and see whose hair has salt in it. If a man owns

salt and carries it to market, some will surely get into his hair. That person will be the true owner." (Remember people carry bundles on their heads.)

The chief looked into Spider's hair and into Opuro's hair, and of course he found the salt in Spider's hair. Therefore, the chief decided that all the salt must belong to Spider.

Poor Opuro! Spider had tricked him. Opuro wanted to get even.

"Spider loves to dance," thought Opuro. "If I give a great dancing party, Spider will be the first to come."

And so, the very next week, Opuro gave a party. He hired special drummers for the dancing, and invited all his friends. Last of all, he sent a special invitation to Spider.

Although Spider received his invitation last, he was the first to come. He came early so he would get plenty to eat. At last, it was time to begin the dancing. The hornblowers blew their horns. The drummers drummed loudly so that people would know something special was going to happen. Then there was silence. Everyone waited.

Opuro walked out in front of the crowd of people. He took some magic medicine from a pot and rubbed it first on one hand and then on the other. Then he rubbed some on his feet. Next, he signaled the drummers to begin again. And Opuro began to dance all by himself. Suddenly something most remarkable happened. Opuro began to float up into the air! Up, up he went, higher and higher, until he was as high as a tall palm tree. And all the time, he kept right on dancing! Opuro was dancing in the middle of the air!

All the people thought it was wonderful. They wondered what kind of magic medicine Opuro possessed. For a long time they stood and watched him dancing up there in the air, and when he came down, everyone clapped.

As for Spider, he was as jealous as he was greedy. His eyes popped open. He turned blue. He nearly choked with envy. He must have some of this wonderful medicine for himself!

"Please, Opuro, please give me some of the medicine," he begged. "I will see that nothing happens to your salt again. Perhaps I could even get some of it back for you."

Opuro gave Spider some of the magic medicine most willingly. He was all smiles.

Of course, Spider immediately planned to have a dancing party of his own. He invited everyone in the village. When everyone was there, Spider rubbed the medicine on his hands and feet, just as Opuro had done. Sure enough, the magic worked! Spider floated up into the air. His feet moved gracefully in the steps of

a dance, just as if he were still on the ground. He was delighted! He stepped delicately this way and that, bowing his head. Spider was dancing in the air, with all the people looking at him. What fun! He shook himself a little and closed his eyes. When he opened them, he was as high as the tallest silk-cotton tree. At once, he was ready to come down again.

Good gracious! He did not know how to get down! He had forgotten to ask Opuro for the rest of the magic secret.

"Help! Get me down," Spider screamed to Opuro, but Opuro only waved at him and laughed. So Spider kept right on going up — far, far into the blue sky, where no one could see him any more.

Spider kept on floating through the air. He floated across the sea and over high mountains. On and on he went — on and on and all the way to England!

It was winter in England and cold. Spider did not like winter. He wanted to get back to

Ashanti, but how could he do it? If only he could make a thread and drop himself across the world!

Spider tried several times. At last, *he spun a thread!* It was fine and silky. It was the world's first spider web. It took him all the way back to Ashanti. When he arrived, people saw the wonderful shining silver thread. They decided to make one like it. From that they learned how to spin thread. Then they looked at the beautiful web Spider wove from his thread. They copied that too, and thus people learned to weave kente.

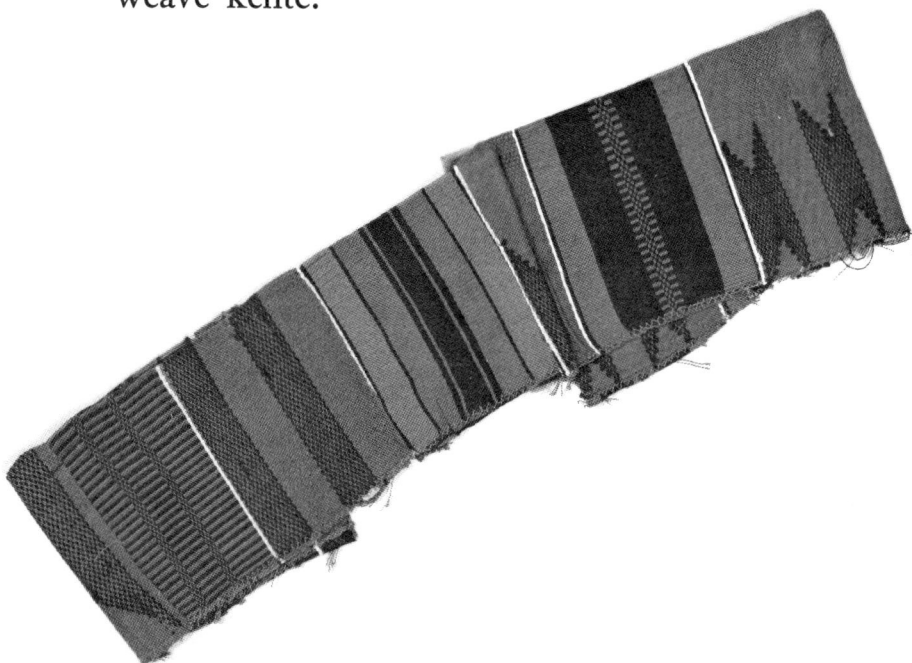

Why Spiders Live in the Ceiling

ONCE upon a time Osebo (that is the name of Leopard) owned a very special kind of sheep. It was a magic sheep. It was magic because, if you lifted it in your arms and held it over a cooking pot, it would fill the pot with fufu. (That is the name of the dumplings that go in an African stew.)

Now, in Ashanti, where Spider lived, everyone loved to eat fufu. And Spider loved it most of all. Spider loved to eat everything, but he was *especially* fond of fufu. And so, when he heard about the magic sheep who could fill a pot with fufu, Spider knitted his brows. "I must get that sheep for myself," he said.

That is how it happened that one evening Spider went to visit Osebo the Leopard.

Osebo received him most politely. He gave Spider some dinner, and the two of them sat talking until the great round moon came up. At last, it was so late that Osebo invited Spider to stay the whole night in his house, and that was *just* what Spider wanted.

"Don't bother to prepare a special bed for me," said Spider pleasantly. "I will just sleep in the kitchen." (He knew the magic sheep always slept in the kitchen.)

"Nonsense," replied Osebo, "I cannot be so rude as to put a guest in the kitchen. Besides, you would have to sleep with my sheep, for she always sleeps in the kitchen."

"Oh, that's all right," answered Spider. "I am used to sleeping with sheep, and I really would not mind it at all."

Again, Leopard refused, but Spider insisted. "I am used to sleeping with sheep, I tell you.

In fact, I *always* sleep with sheep. It is my habit," he cried.

Osebo looked hard at Spider. He was not nearly so stupid as Spider thought he was.

"Very well," Osebo said quietly. "You may sleep in the kitchen."

He laid out a sleeping mat for Spider near the fire and gave Spider a blanket to cover himself. The sheep lay asleep in a corner.

"This is most comfortable," said Spider, as he lay down. He closed his eyes tightly and pretended to go to sleep. As soon as Osebo left the room, Spider crept with his bed into the corner, next to the magic sheep. Spider tried hard to stay awake, but he could not keep his eyes open. Was it the warm fire, or was it the big dinner Spider had eaten? No one knows, but soon Spider was sound asleep.

Now all this time, Osebo was watching. The moment Spider fell asleep, he went into the kitchen. His padded feet made no sound. He lifted up the magic sheep and carried it out of the room. In its place, he put his son, Little Leopard, next to the bed of Spider. And then Osebo quietly blew out the lantern.

Just before daybreak, Spider woke up. He reached out to touch the sheep. Sure enough! He felt the furry body of an animal. Quickly he stuffed it into a large bag he had hidden under his pillow. And then he ran home, with the bag hanging over his shoulder.

Spider was delighted with himself!

When he reached his house, Spider called his wife, Aso, and his son, Kuma. He told them about the wonderful sheep in the bag, for they loved fufu as much as he did.

"Open the bag," they cried.

So Spider opened the bag to show them. What a surprise! Instead of a magic sheep, they saw the great green eyes of a leopard! His teeth were long and sharp, and his claws stuck out like knives.

Spider and his family were so frightened that they dug a tunnel right then and there and ran into it. Little Leopard picked up some magic stones. He threw them at the Spider family and hit their feet as they ran. Spider and Aso and Kuma cried out. Little Leopard ran after them through the tunnel. He was getting closer and closer.

At last the three spiders could run no farther. They burst from the tunnel and climbed high up into the ceiling. They liked it there. They felt warm and safe. And so they decided to stay. If you look carefully, you may find them there now.

How the Moon Came to Be in the Sky

Spider had six fine sons. Each one of them had a special talent — something he could do better than anyone else in the world. And each one was named after this special thing he could do well.

The first son was called *See Trouble*. That was because he could tell when trouble was coming, even from very far away.

The second son was *Road Builder*.

The third was *Able to Drink Up Rivers,* and we will call him *River Drinker*.

The fourth son of Spider was *Skinner of Game*. He was a hunter, and we shall call him *Game Skinner*.

The fifth son was *Stone Thrower*. The sixth son was *Lie on the Ground Soft as a Cushion.* Shall we call him simply *Cushion?*

Here they are, the six sons of Spider:

See Trouble	Game Skinner
Road Builder	Stone Thrower
River Drinker	Cushion

ONE DAY, in the middle of the dry season, Spider went on a long journey. He walked through the green forest and swam across the dark blue rivers. He cooled himself in the shade of the great trees and in the waters of the rivers.

Many days passed. At last, the end of the dry season came. But Spider did not return. His six sons began to worry about him. What had happened to Spider? They loved their father, and they did not want him to be caught in the forest when the heavy rains came.

"We have six special talents," said one of the sons. "Let us put them together so that we may find our father."

And so the next evening the six sons of Spider met in the palaver house.

The first to speak was See Trouble — he who could see trouble a long way off.

"Ah!" he cried, "I see that Father has fallen into a deep river. A big fish has swallowed him. Now he lies in the belly of the fish."

The six sons hurried into the forest to rescue Spider. Road Builder made a road quickly through the forest, and the brothers ran to the spot where Spider had fallen into the water. How could they find the fish? River Drinker swallowed every drop of the river and dried it up, and there, on the bottom lay a great fish. Now Game Skinner took his sharp knife and skinned the fish in a twinkling. At once, Spider jumped out, alive and well as ever.

Spider and his six sons were overjoyed. They all set out for home. But more trouble was coming! A great falcon saw them from the sky. He swooped down and caught Spider in his sharp talons. He carried Spider far, far up into the sky where his six sons could hardly see him.

Stone Thrower picked up a large stone. He threw it at the great bird and hit it. The falcon dropped Spider. Down, down he fell toward the earth below. Cushion spread himself out on the ground, and Spider fell onto his son's great, soft tummy. It was like landing on a bag of feathers. Again, Spider was saved.

Many days later, Spider was walking in the forest. Suddenly he noticed a soft light glowing among the leaves of a lacy fern. He went close to it. It was a beautiful ball of pale silver, and it spread a gentle glow all around it.

"How lovely!" exclaimed Spider. "I will give this light to the son who helped me most when I was in danger. It is a perfect prize."

And so, Spider prayed to Nyame, the God

of the Sky, to come down and hold the shining ball until he could decide which of his sons deserved it most. Nyame heard and came. He held the silvery ball in his right hand, and waited for Spider to choose the son who should receive it. But *there* was the problem! Which son deserved the prize? Spider could not decide. Each one had helped Spider in his own way.

After many days, Nyame grew tired of waiting for Spider to make up his mind. He rose slowly up into the heavens, taking the lovely light with him. He placed it there in the sky of night for all men to see. It is shining there still. Have you seen it?